for Cindy
Birthday

THE GIFT OF MANTRA

❁ ❁ ❁

by Tom Pinkson, Ph.D

a 7th Direction production for Wakan Publishing

dedication

This book is dedicated to my three grandsons,
Corbin, Luke and Sebastian,
who fill me with joy with their presence.

May they each find their own mantras to enliven their lives
and fulfill their highest potentials for a meaningful life.

May it also be so for all who find their way to this book.

And gratitude to Roger Clay, producer of this book,
for his patience, artistry and skill.

ISBN: 978-0-9984156-0-4

Book design, image processing and layout by
7th Direction Productions
Novato California
info@7thdirection.com

Front and Rear Cover Yarn Painting art by Mariano Valadez

It's a daunting task to keep the heart open and the mind clear when facing the challenges of daily life. Mantras, short phrases or sentences repeated out loud, sung or voiced in silence have been used by peoples around the world throughout time to focus awareness on an uplifting thought.

Visualizing the meaning of the mantra helps activate a flow of healing energy that uplifts the spirit and promotes wellbeing. Self-made mantras can be tailored to the specifics of whatever qualities of mind and emotional state you wish to experience thereby enriching your life experience. All you need to make it happen is your self and your creative imagination.

What follows in this book are some mantras and phrases coupled with images that can open doorways to spiritual communion with your heart and soul. I use different ones every day depending upon my mood. As you page through this book, when a mantra sparks a connection, I invite you to explore it as a practical tool by using it to start your day, through the course of the day and upon ending the day.

~ Tom Pinkson - San Anselmo, California, 2016

Wake Up! Wake Up!
Remember
Who you are

We are Sacred, Worthy Luminous Beings

We are love and our love is for giving

Fullest Blossoming
Greatest Good

Truth of Wisdom
Wisdom of Truth

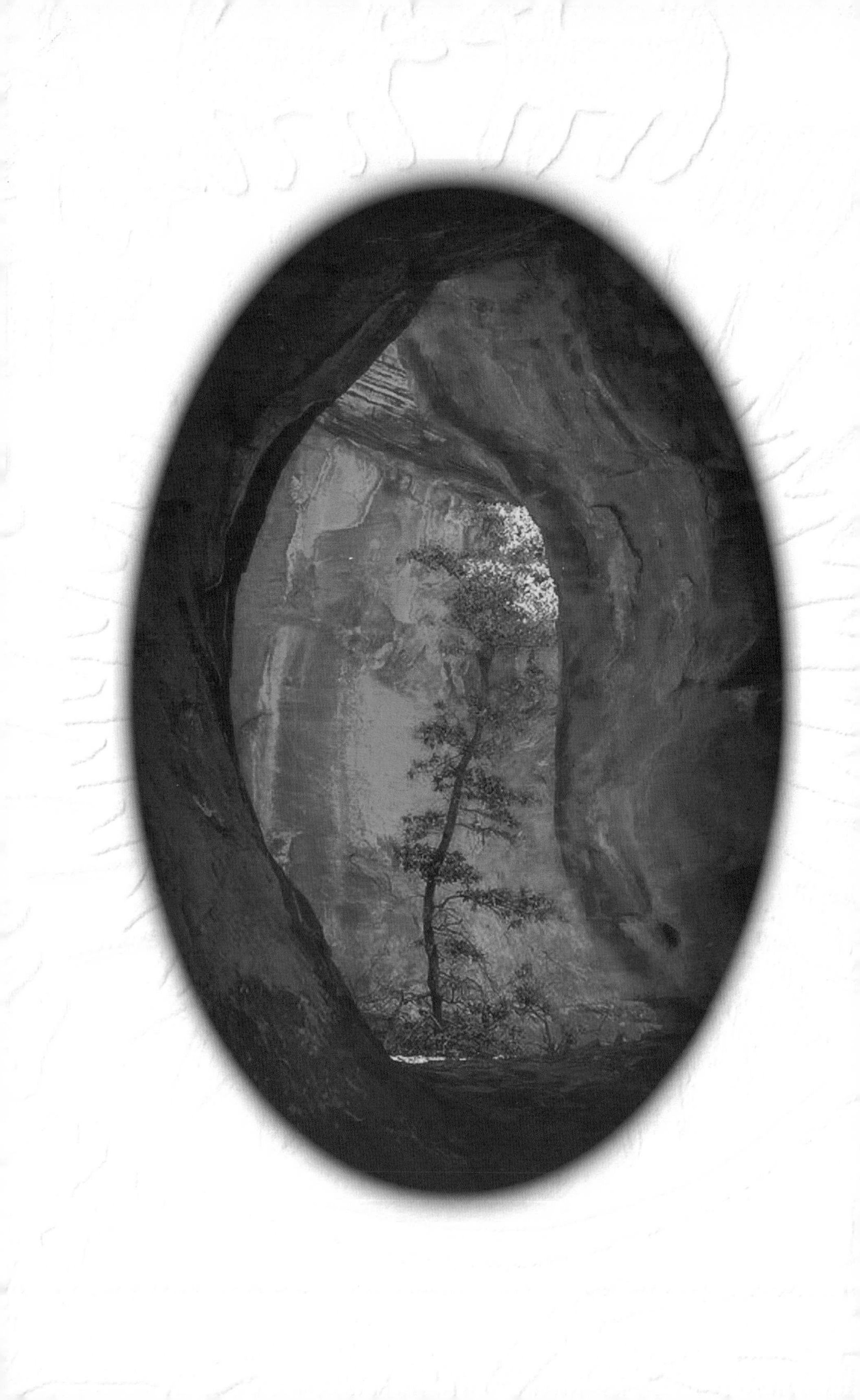

What gets in the way,
is the Way

When the going gets tough, you get what you practice

Remember to surrender
Surrender to remember

Peace abides
Wisdom guides
Love provides

Fierce With Kindness

Kind with Fierceness

It's not about seeing new things.
It's about seeing with new eyes.

There's magic in the ordinary.
It's all around.
There's magic in the ordinary,
waiting to be found

**I carry my heart through this world,
like a Life-Giving Sun.
Shining so bright, on each and every one**

It's all about relationship
The web we weave so fine
It's all about relationship
The love we have to shine

Painting by Michelle Gold

!! Coyote Alert !!

Perhaps you're dreaming too small!

Safe
Faith
Go slow
Joy will follow

I choose to experience inner peace, now

Where there is darkness
let there be Light!

Love is the key
Let its medicine do me

Make a good home for the Ancestor Spirits

I set my sails to catch the breeze of God's Grace

Let Love Live
Let it flow
Let it grow

Everthing we say, think, feel and do ripples outward

Oneness
Flow
Gratitude

Infinite Light is what I see.
Infinite Love is what I be!

“Remove your shoes from your feet for the place you stand upon is holy ground”

Grace grows where gratitude flows

❁ ❁ ❁

Peace of Patience Patience of Peace

❁ ❁ ❁

Find the holiness in all things.

Love is the glue that holds us together

Old Ones, Old ones
Tell your ancient stories
so your wisdom can live on

Walk on a Heart Path to completion

Nature bats last

Artwork by Rohmana D'Arezzo George

**In the cosmic dance of life
you are not here by accident
but with Divine Purpose**

Saying adios, for now, dear reader.
May your ceremonies grow and flow.

All Blessings – All-Ways.

Tomás

ABOUT THE AUTHOR

Tom Pinkson, aka, tomás, is a Ph.D. psychologist, author, ceremonial retreat and vision-fast leader, sacred storyteller and musician who completed an eleven year apprenticeship with Huichol shamans in Mexico. He helped start the first live-in hospice in the United States and worked for 32 years with terminally ill children at the Center for Attitudinal Healing in California, successfully integrating the wisdom teachings of indigenous spirituality into the world of the practicing psychologist.

He is the founder of Wakan, a nonprofit organization committed to restoring the sacred in daily life. Tom helps people wake up and connect to their deeper, authentic being remembering they are sacred, worthy, luminous beings; they are love and their love is for giving

Tom resides in northern California with Andrea, his wife of fifty years, and enjoys the company of his two daughters, their husbands and three grandsons all living nearby.

An Open Invitation:

One of the intentions of this book is to inspire you to create your own mantras. I welcome and encourage you to send me any good ones you come up with and, with your permission of course, we'll share them with others on my Facebook page.

Here are some ways for us to stay connected:

Email: tompinkson@gmail.com

Websites and Social Media:

www.drtompinkson.com
www.nierica.com
www.facebook.com/SacredLiving

...and visit my on-line store at:

http://drtompinkson.com/shop/